UNIVERSITY OF CALGARY
Press

W0037708

The *High Line*
Scavenger Hunt

LUCAS CRAWFORD

Brave & Brilliant Series
ISSN 2371-7238 (Print) ISSN 2371-7246 (Online)

University of Calgary Press
2500 University Drive NW
Calgary, Alberta
Canada T2N 1N4
press.ucalgary.ca

This book is available as an ebook. The publisher should be contacted for any use which falls outside the terms of that license.

LIBRARY AND ARCHIVES CANADA CATALOGUING IN PUBLICATION

Crawford, Lucas, 1983-, author
    The high line scavenger hunt / Lucas Crawford.

(Brave & brilliant series, 2371-7238 ; no. 7)
Poems.
Issued in print and electronic formats.
ISBN 978-1-77385-000-9 (softcover).—ISBN 978-1-77385-001-6 (PDF).—
ISBN 978-1-77385-002-3 (EPUB).—ISBN 978-1-77385-003-0 (Kindle)

    I. Title. II. Series: Brave & brilliant series ; 7

PS8605.R43H55 2018   C811'.6   C2018-904053-X
                                             C2018-904054-8

The University of Calgary Press acknowledges the support of the Government of Alberta through the Alberta Media Fund for our publications. We acknowledge the financial support of the Government of Canada. We acknowledge the financial support of the Canada Council for the Arts for our publishing program.

Canada Council   Conseil des Arts
for the Arts   du Canada

Printed and bound in Canada by Marquis
♻ This book is printed on 70 lb Rolland Opaque Smooth Natural paper

Editing by Helen Hajnoczky
Cover illustration: Melina Cusano, *The HL for Lucas*, 2018, watercolour, pen and ink
Cover design, page design, and typesetting by Melina Cusano

The High Line
Scavenger Hunt

Table of Contents

Think Like an Architect!

At Columbia University's
"Introduction to Architecture" intensive,
there were two students who had troubles:
—me, fey with gay wrists, summer-flushed and sweating.
—him, buzzcut and ambulating arhythmically
to the beat of a palsied drum.

Not one person would help us screw together
our drafting boards with a drill,
so he held the drill   gyratory hand like a dancer
I held the screw   timorous hand held out as if
                            I awaited a strap.

At the Crit, he showed us his collage of the High Line:
walkways cut and pasted into the quavers of his gait.
My all-thumbs first attempt was a collage about
washrooms, the meat market, transgender history.

The TA scolded us:
well you've got to ask yourself
who am I to decide
what patrons of a building
should have to think about?

I went searching for a deserted bathroom to use.
My friend nodded, went off to find a ramp.

Next assignment, I cursed it all:
Chopped at photos like a butcher
Smeared gluestick here or there
Slapped traces down where they fell.

1

The professor held it, smiled,
and delivered her evaluation:

NOW you're starting to think like an architect!

Summer 2009, Manhattan

Architecture fails
you this summer.

Your roof collapses on you and your visitor.
Brain damage. The ER. The black eyes.

The fridge makes everything smell of rot.
Resort to bananas and wax-wrapped cheese.

The ivy league summer studio in Architecture teaches you
why there aren't more transgender or disabled architects.

[If you cannot work twenty hours a day,
abusing the curvature of the spine
with a medieval torture device
known as a drafting table,

and survive on vending machine cheese curls,
and learn to use the tools yourself,
and stop talking about gender,
and forget history,

then you do not
deserve to design
stairwells for
corporate clients!]

Stay up nights writing what you think is your thesis.
Jam up your lower back in the butt-hugging fabric chair
at the desk in your room in the overpriced apartment in the city
that feels for country-you like the edge of the world.

Doormen disallow your entry to the chiropractor's office.
Scavenge dimes for a phone call. Let yourself be out of joint.

You have been Lucas for a year now,
but don't expect it to feel regular yet.
[I've just celebrated ten years!
The red velvet cake was scrumptious. If bloody.]

Get distracted in studio and slice off your fingertip.
Again, the ER. Wandering high. Fly away.

The see-saws of tipping points
will jerk you as would the sea.
Don't fret, this next decade, about who
you suspect others may think you ought to be.

These are hard years; let's not lie.
You will not avoid the party game
in which guests strive to
pin an essence to your "I."

Avert your eyes. Say some goodbyes.
Look awry; look around. Live
in a haunted mansion on the
dead-end edge of a prairie town.

Be everyone.
Be nobody.

Don't be
settled down.

I.
A Bone, A Tooth, A Ghost

Flagging Red

Before the High Line was built,
the train sliced through traffic at street level,
a sword swung through the body politic.
The train sometimes (too often) killed those
who were cavalier about jaywalking
or running the amber   before there *was* an amber.

Eventually, someone tried to sheath this sword
with just a warning, just an older style
of controlling herds:
men on horseback were hired to precede each train,
to blow a horn or wave a red flag by light, and
to hold a red lantern by night.

I like to pretend that one of these "West-Side Cowboys"
        retired early with a sore hip,
        cut the buttocks out of his chaps,
        rubbed some rouge onto his cheeks,
        folded his red flag into a tight square,
        tucked it into his back right pocket and
        strolled into a meat market watering hole, thinking:
                Honey, let's do *something with this place.*

Honey, Let's *Do* Something with This Place

But there are no innocents.
No pioneer spirit makes right.

When my head hits pillow, I wonder what
the west-side cowboys dreamt of at night.

A bottom bent over for a
leather man wielding a whip.

A cure for his sore hip and
his urban cowboy depression.

A minor in the history of land dispossession.
A $300 per hour psychoanalysis session.

A date with a man at a delicatessen.
Smoked meat, wry smiles, and mustard.

Or is it his father
wielding a whip,

or, any father holding manhood
with an iron-fisted tight grip?

Sorrows of the West-Side Cowboy

Woe is he who brings only the news of oncoming
noise-nuisance. He is the harbinger, the forbearer,
the premature panic button, the premonition, the broken spirit
that breaks horses and signifies the coming
of something heavy. He is a token of the dangerous future
and a clip-clop *memento mori* in the distance.

> *Oh, but sweetheart, I just*
> *smile when I see you coming.*

Woe is he who used to scarf pemmican astride a horse
and now munches on minced tongue and butter sandwiches
at a table during break. Is he nostalgic about that stolen
Native American recipe of marrow and meat? When you've already
taken so much, it's hard to draw a moral line, isn't it, cowboy?

> *We've been broken like horses, Sugar,*
> *and there are so many reasons to be sour.*

Woe is he whose father gold-rushed in 1897 and lost
two fingers for Klondike cold. You can imagine how his Father
might've felt about the idea of New York City cowboys.
When he hit his son, his son could feel phantom fingers
drumming him, like the way you feel when you
piss or cum in a dream   (you wake dry but
                                         know it happened).

> *Hit snooze, my sweet buckaroo,*
> *and just do that thing you do.*

Woe is he who can see the future—not just a train coming
but also the twenty-first century office-speak dictionary
that defines a "red-flag" as an indicator that a business deal
is *too* sweet. His father says he looks like a runaway
communist, that his flag needs white and blue too.

Forget our fathers, baby, tie up
the horse and be my daddy.

Who is he who spends his days
with a dummy engine hounding his heels?
Who is he who hears horseshoe on steel
each time his teeth hit the dinner fork?
Who is he who will be outmoded by
the sheer uplifting of street into sky?

Him, him, them, us,
me, you, or who?

FOUND: Daily Menu for the West-Side Cowboy on a Moderate Budget

Hungry? Grab a copy of *Mrs. Putnam's Receipt Book: and Young Housekeeper's Assistant* to enjoy these treats circa 1876!

Breakfast

FRIED TOMATOES.
Slice the tomatoes ; dredge on a little flour,
pepper and salt. Fry them in butter for breakfast.

Dinner

STUFFED LOAF.
Mince what is left of a leg of veal ; mix with it pepper, salt,
a little mace, and a little onion if preferred. Take a stale
baker's loaf (an outside one is preferable, as it has more crust) ;
cut a hole about three inches square in the bottom of it,
and scoop out all the soft (this can be saved for a bread-pudding) ;
then, after heating the mince in the spider, fill the loaf with it ;
replace the square piece of crust and tie it up ; then put the loaf
into the spider in hot fat, and turn it over until the whole is a
dark brown. Garnish the dish, and it will be a very
attractive looking ornament for a table.

Dessert

BOILED SUET PUDDING.*
Take a pint of milk, three eggs, and sifted flour enough
to make a thick batter, a cup of suet chopped fine,

and a spoonful of salt ; mix it all together, and boil
four hours. Serve with wine sauce.

Nightly Constitutional

A VERY STRENGTHENING DRINK.
Beat the yolk of a fresh egg with a little sugar ;
add a very little brandy ; beat the white to a strong froth,
stir it into the yolk ; fill up the tumbler with new milk,
and grate in a little nutmeg.

*DIARRHHOEA.
One table-spoonful of flour stirred
into a half a tumbler of water, and drink it ;
and repeat it in a few hours if the first should
not check it. A simple but effectual remedy.

My Death Avenue

Before the elevated High Line was built,
there were so many casualties
of the street-level train that 10th Avenue
was nicknamed Death Avenue.

In 2009, my fate-worse-than-Death
Avenue is not in New York
Or maybe it is sometimes—Wall Street
in drag as somewhere-you-want-to-be.

But really my Death Avenue slips and slides;
it is carpet shaped and flies
with witchery through cold air;
it plants itself onto other streets
like a tick or a banana-peel slapstick trap.

Sometimes Death Avenue manifests before my eyes.
Not much of a Midas Touch, that!
Maybe I'm just Rapunzel-gone-gay   No first born but
                                     spinning gold with my
                                     country toes into hay

Death Avenue can be Edmonton's Whyte Ave,
flanked with gyms filled with guys stuffed with
smoothies chocked with powdered egg white
and too much *Hoo-Rah* hoo-hah

Death Avenue yokes we freaks up to a hundred chariots
with backseat drivers holding quick-draw whips.

Guys, let's not
get physical . . .

On Whyte, we slurped oysters still attached,
umbilical to shell. They were rancid.

On Whyte, we dance-avoided Mormon
recruiters like fat hopscotch champs.

Once, on Whyte, however,
I sidewalk-sat with a drunk-hungry 3 AM friend.

We ate cheap cake with our hands and kissed.
I think of that night when I remember Whyte
and I need a reminder of how to live
between rum breath and death.

Found: On Not Looking Back

*From transphobic / trans-fetishistic reviews of the
High Line Park:*

I used to live nearby the High Line
when the neighborhood was more
Tranny Hooker than Helmut Lang.

Back then, it was hard to imagine
in less than twenty years, the butcher shop
on Washington Street, where split hogs
dangled from ropes, would become a boutique.
The transsexuals moved on, too.

In the 1980s, it was notorious for leather bars
and transsexual streetwalkers. Today,
one can shop at Diane von Furstenberg
and rub elbows with the uber-chic and with
schoolchildren on the High Line.

In the 1980s, I used to work near the High Line
back when it was an abandoned stretch
of rusting steel, sheltering transexual [*sic*] hookers
as they plied their trade to motorists

If you stopped in the bodega on the corner of Horatio and
Washington for your morning bagel and coffee, you might have
found yourself next to a beautiful woman in short skirt and high
platform boots baring a six-pack midriff beneath a leather halter
top, a hint of beard peaking through her pancake makeup

Twenty years ago the only way to be caught
in this neighborhood would have been dead.
With the coming of the long-awaited High Line
this is one neighborhood that's not looking back.

And sitting on the edge of all this, hovering silently
above, like a severed limb, is the High Line.

First Page of an Academic Article in Drag as a Poem

According to the *Lonely Planet Discover New York* guide,
"It's hard to believe that the High Line—
a shining example of brilliant urban renewal—
was once a dingy rail line that anchored
a rather unsavory district of thugs,
trannies and slaughterhouses" (Bonetto et al. 2012).

In this succinct commentary, readers learn
that the new High Line park's significance
may only be grasped through the violence
of a specific juxtaposition with transgender;
one cannot appreciate how far the area has come,
apparently, until one hears about how low it had sunk.

As in other reviews of the park, this means that
"trannies" become the inverse to the High Line, both as
a history that makes the park's popularity "hard to believe"
and as a discursive presence that must continually—
even compulsively—be conjured up and cast out.

The presumed moral dimension of the High Line is clear:
even when it was "dingy," it was an "anchor," as if
its matter held the area's inhabitants from drifting
into the Hudson River by sheer weight and pull.

Now that the railway has been buffed up—it is "shining"—
it is an icon both of the meatpacking district's
cultural cachet and of urban renewal itself.

Bolstered by the ease with which the phrase
"trannies and slaughterhouses" pairs the figure of
the (racialized, class-specific, labouring) transsexual
with death, meat, and outmoded commerce,
the trans history of the meatpacking district becomes
the very antithesis of urban vitality [in this rhetoric].

[...]

... to many people it is not "hard to believe"
that underneath a hip neighborhood
lies a past of marginalized people
or that the gaze of the urban planner or politician
has the alchemical capacity to transform bodies
into social symptoms.

At this juncture, at which the championing of architectural
transition seems to rely on the abjection of transsexual
transition, an opening question is obvious: what gives?

s,l,a,u,g,h,t,e,r,h,o,u,s,e,s, a,n,d, t,r,a,n,s,s,e,x,u,a,l,s

[Can the letters of this violent
juxtaposition be subverted?]

A terse hetero laughs at transsexuals.
These laughs are snares, lugnuts.
He rests, butt on grass, Lotus-legs.
He's host to hot aroused thoughts
although he has gone other routes,
sang other songs, hung onto
other resolute slugs.
(All these hetero louts
long for trans hugs! A
hex on these losers!)

Oh, Eros—that art that
sees roses, hears long last songs,
sets tresses, stresses hearts.

He hangs out here, leers.
He sought to outlast—to oust—
these thoughts, to test
the hetero soul.

Though . . .

He eats a hole, groans. Ears, nose, rear!
The nexuses: head to butt, tongue to testes.
He halts, *stat*, lest he shoot too soon.

Later, he tells tales to sell out
the arousal, the languorous rest.

He's a rooster that hates hen, hates nest.
He's eaten up; he laughs; he's alone.

Next hetero sex role, he hears
slaughter tones, slaughter roast.

The heart steers alone, houses loss.
The ears taste a ghost.

Bills, Bills, Bills

A billboard adjacent to the High Line,
and curated by the High Line staff, displays art.
In December, 2011, the billboard showed
John Baldessari's commissioned work,
The First $100,000 I Ever Made.

This was a stretch-skewed
one hundred-thousand-dollar bill
casting a cash shadow onto
a changed 10TH Avenue.

Forty-two thousand of the real-deal big-bills
were sent to Federal Reserve Banks
during a three-week episode
that straddled 1934 and 1935.

They were recalled in the 1960s, before recalls
were caused by hysteria about meat market salmonella
or by lysteria monocytogenes in raw-milk cheese
found a thirteen-hour train ride away in Quebec.

Recalled because wire transfers
made them more obsolete
than the penny.

Most were destroyed—
by fire? by shredder? by origami? collage?
where are the ashes? the confetti? crafts?

A few remain, with glass
between us and them
at the Smithsonian.
Rubble-relics
relegated to collections
curated as tightly as a bank account.

Chaucer's Pardoner could turn a good trick
peddling these tokens on the upper east side
But the bills already were the fake bones of a saint,
vouchers to encourage economic ventures,
down-paymenting a future
fabricating faith where none—

the art and artwork of
proclaiming a past by fiat.

Things to Buy with a One Hundred Thousand Dollar Bill

Doubled wages for four point one-six-five
Canadians living on the poverty line.

Twenty-five thousand Subway roundtrips
to and from work in Manhattan.

Tuition for two years of Columbia Law School
for an American student.

Two million penny candies
(they cost five cents now).

Two hundred and fifty heavy-
duty adult tricycles.

Weekly dinner for four at Le Cirque for two years.
72, 049 tubs of Gerber's Peas baby food.

Four years of medical health care costs for one HIV+ person.
Housing cost for a two-year prison sentence.

4545.45454545454545454545454545
official High Line onesies.

Two years + two months of rent for a one-bedroom
apartment at the Highline condos.

Ninety-three weekend stays at the Standard Hotel
that sits atop the High Line.

Surgical procedures for seven transgender women or five transgender men (approx.).

0.5% of the donation adjacent retailer Diane von Furstenberg made to the High Line.

Redwood Wall

The graffiti near the High Line is drab-gray gone.
Institutional shades cover up pasts like mad.

My friend Jay once fell from a tree while tagging a wall.
He landed in an improperly secured barrel of fat at McDonald's.
I don't know if this contravened his vegan diet by osmosis
or if his art is premised on any lie of purity or permanence.

The graffiti near the High Line is drab-gray gone.

They didn't scrub those walls; the paint remains.
The paint, like guilt, is repressed, is shellacked
under another new fleeting surface.

Institutional shades cover up pasts like mad.

Old walls grow forward
The patina encroaches outwards
like bark on a tree. You could cut
a cross-section of this wall
and count the rings.

This is another way
of learning to tell time.

Vestigial Limbs, 1980

With three last carloads of frozen turkeys
chugging down the rails, the High Line
became a dead duck—a bird that can't fly
a trainless track
a gravy boat.

Those turkeys once looked up to a tree and thought
I think I can I think I can I think I can but they couldn't

Those train cars?
Filled with dead architectures of bones
still flesh-bound   Those bones? Simmered
                           with mirepoix, sage, and thyme

Somebody must have cried over this last run:
a conductor on his premature last shift, or,
a renter joyous for a night of sleep;
without her toothbrush jittering in its glass.
Somebody cried and the wealthy
season popcorn with the salt.

A man lorded over a table in Chelsea
wielding an electric carving knife
White meat? Dark meat? White meat? Dark meat?
The track always loops back to colour and flesh.

He did not need to imagine that someday many people
would wrap their collective pinkie fingers around the train
that brought him his turkey   and would then pull
on the count of three   making a wish

Promenade Plantée 1

In Paris, there is an elevated parkway that
some people call "the original High Line,"
as if Paris is just a footnote or forerunner.

The first grand defunct railroad-park has a pet name:
la Coulée Vert [The Green Flow]

The path slices through the 12TH arrondisement, even,
at one point, seeming to cut a building clear apart.

> It winds by a dozen replica statues
> of Michelangelo's *The Dying Slave*:
> a man with a cloth-wrapped torso
> and one hand tied behind his back.
>
> They were hammered out for a Pope's tomb
> and now they sit atop a police station.
>
> From afar, they look like a line of yawning
> transgender men with bound chests.

Promenade Plantée II

The promenade passes by the Bastille.
I imagine a visitor on this spot, conjuring up

a dozen of those clothbound-man
statues of grey-green hue,

with their hands tied behind their backs
by a master sculptor,

with the strength and patience
of their bratty submissive selves,

having now been
magic-spelled alive

as they storm the High Line,
taking over the Paris police,
breaking black bars
with marble force.

Just when a slippery hand of law
gets a cuff around a statue's wrist
all twelve liquidize, ooze
into the park's water feature.

They infuse the High Line
with the gloss-green glow
of malachite rock, old moss
faded bills, and envy.

Promenade Plantée III

Promenade Plantée,
Public Park (Paris).

People pushed *pour* pine-pumped praiseworthy promenade;
Paris planned popular park. Postoperative,
Promenade Plantée prevails peerless.
People *prends* photos, prolific piles.

Planes pull past Poseidon's pond;
passengers pack pell-mell;
pilots puff pall-malls.
People purr paeans pour pioneers.
Paintings portray Plymouth pebble.

Populace "preserves" plagued packing-precinct.
Police plug pesky proletariat pleasures ("protection").
Planners proffer prolepsis,
preemptively prevent possible protest.

Planners proselytize, pontificate,
perform posh *parôles* promoting profit.
Phlegmatic park planners
prompt passionate paternalism,
piss-pickle public perceptions, pictures, personifications.
Planners praise "providence."

People park-play
produce pharmaceuticals
pursue psychoanalysis
perform physiques
push paleo.

Post-Paris packing-precinct park
prohibits polyamorous play,
prohibits posterior pinching
 (perennial perversions personifying plural pasts,
 progenitor prehistories, profane pedigrees,
 prematurely perished prizefighters).

Paris postmodern park pauperized. (Promenade Plantée,
passé?) Paris presently possesses *penultimate* promenade?
(Phony portrayal . . .)

Parcontre, people perpetually prefer Paris pastries
Plats principaux pigout: *potage petit pois,
porc, poisson, poivres, parfait.*

  Puis, populations progressively plan planted pathways.
  Prochain: Philadelphia, Pennsylvania.

The Mineshaft 1

The Mineshaft (1976-1985) was an exclusive—nay,
exclusionary—gay men's kink club in the meat market.

My chromosomes would have no home here
and my junk would be garbage to them.

I'd not be admitted here, but I confess
that my body might have been there.

> My great uncle died in a mine and I aim for
> subtext, try to dig deep to the underground.

> The Mineshaft is another place I haven't been
> that might just be built of my ruins:

Ribcage, its downstairs jail cell;
my kinked intestines, a pile of rope.

Ass, the club's wide bath for piss; rectum,
a wide berth for the bullshit of exclusion.

I don't care that I have no
shaft for The Mineshaft.

The sphincter through which chewed food
passes to duodenum is my glory hole.

This is just another place I haven't been
that a less ambivalent queer

might get inked on their
High Line sun-sunken skin.

The lower floor had a dungeon and
red-blooded jail cells filled with men

who were hard and soft enough to drive
each particle of you to self-syncopate,

to slip the double-walled protective sac
off your heart quicker than a full condom.

When I try to picture The Mineshaft
I squint so hard I see only dark, but

when I look askance, a fist
unfolds and crosses fingers.

FOUND: The Mineshaft's Dress Code

Approved items in the Mineshaft Dress Code
as originally adopted are:

- leather cycle styles
- western gear
- levis
- T-Shirts
- tanktops
- official uniforms
- plaid and plain shirts
- some rugged workpants
- cut offs
- gymwear
- jockstraps
- and
- just plain sweat.

Those items
<u>not</u> approved are:

- those which do not fit in a man's club
  where visions of leather, cowboys, uniforms
  and jocks are a reality and not just
  sugar plums at Christmas.

In other words:

- <u>NO</u> COLOGNE, PERFUME,
  OR STRONG AFTERSHAVE

- <u>NO</u> SUITS, TIES, JACKETS,
  DRESS PANTS, OR FANCY SHIRTS

- <u>NO</u> DISCO DRAG, NO MAKE-UP
  OR FEMININE HAIR STYLES

- <u>NO</u> FANCY DESIGNER SWEATERS

- <u>NO</u> RUGBY OR OTHER STRIPED SHIRTS

- <u>NO</u> HEAVY OUTERWEAR OR PARKAS

and, last but not least, LA COSTE STYLE SHIRTS.
(This is a <u>NO NO</u>, even if manufactured by those
who ignore the original alligator and replace it
with foxes, sailboats, pigs or monograms.)

Dress Code Infractions

To be nostalgic about a club that would
not have admitted you takes chutzpa.

Every soft limb of me and mine
would be a lump of coal in the stocking

of the round bearded man checking his list
twice at the door of The Mineshaft.

At times, my neck smells like harvest vineyard,
perfume on my wrist is "At the Beach 1966."

My cyan faux silk shirt has plastic diamond buttons;
my brown tie bursts with orange freckles.

> Alligator shirts or not
> Dress codes are a crock

Chirping about our jewelry
Comparing gender rubble

Unmasked and back-lashed,
we still fly in, unawares, are still

the canaries in
The Mineshaft.

How could a skid of eyeliner mar your night? Or tresses
that tease the collar, or dicks you don't understand or

flaccid matter pinned back
tight as a ballerina's bun?

Leave it to the men baptizing in
a tub of piss to be judgmental—

their wounds whispered into us
in a rotary-age telephone game,

severed
cord.

Is this violence known,
in other worlds, as kin?

The Mineshaft II

THEORY: The Mineshaft can function as a symbol for a space-based gayness premised on the rejection of many.

OBSERVATION: The Mineshaft is gone for violent reasons but the scars of its own violence persist in other places.

QUESTION: how does one hold an animal that is injured and wants to injure you?

FEELING 1: Anomie.

FEELING 2: Boundlessness.

FINAL EXAM: Draw a picture of the void.

BONUS QUESTION: Can you go on?

R.I.D. (A Response to *Residents in Distress*, a late 1990s Neighbourhood Watch Group)

Recalcitrant rabble-rousers, rowdy room renters,
rouge roadway dames, irritate immature doctors.

Rich residents reject rap, repel raunch insistently,
rail incessantly, distort dusk-doings, detest drag,
dumbly influence (indeed, ratify) rezoning drafts.

Dentists invest dollars in Iraq, in immunodeficiency drugs.
Realtors install royal dynasties, drive Rolls-Royces.

Intruders inscribe imposter initiatives in rock:
reclaim rightful roadways, routes, drives!

Irksome republicans;
immoral democrat rats.

Distressed residents remain
race-dumb. Inequality renewed.

Rebels issue retorts; deliver radio reports; defend
resistant dreams, imagine imperfect dialogue; interject
rational debate; isolate institutional racism; do drag.

Ironic representations do damage, irking duped interlopers.
Dramatic irony reveals inconsistencies in
impenetrable doublespeak. Radical diction.

I rewrite intuitive rhymes. Iambic? Dactylic?
Inexact rhythm destabilizes intuitions, revs imagination.
Does it incite rapt interest in redeveloping revolutionary idioms?

> Itchy rash? Rally round irreparable railway.
> Reclaim downtrodden railroad real estate!
> Design recreational refuge!
> *Reincarnation! Rescue! Renovate!*
> Donate dollars. Rub railway raw.

Rinse.
Repeat.

Repent?

Surprise Lice-Check Day at Elementary School

Pubescent panic: I don't know how to redo my ponytail after
the school's volunteer loosens me up to inspect my scalp.
(The punishments for failed femininity
have been greatly underestimated.)

A few kids disappear for a fortnight
Come back scrub-a-dubbed and mumbling:
when you finally kill them,
a new generation is already incubating.

Were we this precocious with language? If so, was it a salve?
My scalp was an A+. This doesn't mean it didn't sting. Double
negativity is not my middle name but I know
that surviving poison doesn't not hurt.

It is *we* who are conceived in
an immaculate parasite orgy
in the corner of the attic
where you're afraid to go alone.

II.
A Blueprint, A Blade, A Branch

Metamorphosis

27 July 2011: crates of butterflies
are released on the High Line.

As instinct ushers the moth to a midnight cigarette,
parents deliver children to the monarch liberation.

      I'm more attracted to beautiful things
      becoming vermin.

When I lose myself, I rewind words
like stray yarn around the skein.
Is it possible for a butterfly to flap backwards?
Would it turn back time?

I have a troubled dream that
every bridge grew into a park.
I am on the North side of the river
and my loves are on the South.

      A travelling salesman sells me
      a very small boat with one oar and says

      the circuitous route
      leads to the centre of things

20 July 2011: they let fly 3500 ladybugs.
The children are learning a lot.

The High Line and I Aren't Men

We both have repurposed, reused, recycled limbs
Limbs we've sent off the rails with force
Force stronger than steam locomotion
A boiling kettle hisses: *come on baby*
                    let's off-road to the ocean

Used-up limbs are fine
because the High Line and I don't abide
by crow-fly time. We live in déjà vu
for the very first time   time
Slow as almost quitting time   time
Fast as a dime placed on the tracks   time
                    and just as
                    warped afterwards

If you pull back a frond or two of our skin,
we will collapse, drop, ooze.

We disappear into drainage grates
and what's left will stick to your shoes.

We are pomegranates, sweet but
you'll be spitting hard seed
(Not a semen reference
because the High Line and I   ARE NOT MEN)

Each seed of us, each *aril*, is a month or a year.
All the High Line and I are is time, absorbed.
But it is not certain that we even have insides

The High Line and I aren't men.
We do not play tug-of-war with other men
or with those parts of us
about which one might say   *it takes one to know one . . .*

Feel it for Yourself

Walk the High Line:
trace your toe along
every dotted scissor-cut line
every piece of scrubbed-up
collaged piece of the Hudson Line.
Put your ear to shallow turf to hear
the ocean or a conductor's ghost.

The High Line's body says:
I've already been dead, dude, and now
I'M THIS. I don't know for how long.

Visit the High Line after hours.
Scale the side like punks used to—
cricket-quick—
to lie on your back in the thicket.

With your right hand,
rub every mark of time on your body
thumbing through your archive.

With your left, stroke the old tracks
they've inserted into the sidewalk.
Stroke the old tracks that cut
across the High Line's chest

        like the scars
        I don't have.

FOUND: Selected Plant Species on the High Line Park

Sunburst   Red Sprite
Shadbush   Crabapple

Black Gum   Nannyberry
European Hornbeam
American Cranberry

        Handsome Harry
        Bottlebrush Buckeye
        Allegheny Serviceberry

        Creeping Raspberry
        Common Quaking Grass
        Bunny Blue Spreading Sedge
        Drooping Star of Bethlehem

Sea Lavender   Umbrella Magnolia
Hula Dancer Pale Purple Coneflower
Winter Sun Mahonia

Ornamental Onion   Sunburst
Striped Squil   Summersweet

Blackhaw Virburnum Leatherleaf Spurge
Blue Ice Bluestar   Pink Lily Leek   Limelight

Hummelo Hudgenettle
Foamflower   Fringetree

Desert False Indigo
          Showy Tick-Trefoil
          Abbeville Blue Chaste Tree
          Midwinter Fire Bloodtwig Dogwood

Fumewort
Eastern Beebalm
Lesser Calamint
Superba Tufted Fescue

                    Pearly Everlasting
                    Bitter Panic Grass

Huddle, 24 May 2012

Today on the High Line
dancers will reprise
Simone Forti's
1961 group dance
performance:

a tight slow mass
of bodies will seep
down the High Line
One by one, each will break
off from the group
elevate itself, rise
like a drawbridge
atop the huddle
and melt back in, into
the centre of things

       Bodies and train tracks can
both morph like this too.
A hot gust rises and a draft
     sneaks in at an oblique angle
A set of sore shoulders
     inflates and exhumes
A clock's second hand fights
     upwards, falls down slower

     Today on the High Line, history   again
     The self-same story of a limb
     that rises, falls, rises   again
        but never   again
        like this

Lounging, Wood

The long wooden loungers
are not assembled into
monogamous twos
or nuclear fours.

They are big, even fat;
I can take my wide load off.
Lying with my friend Coral,
halving a squash muffin,
the crumbs are wind-flung
like mites' kites and we
hug for warmth on this
February visit that is
framed by hard
piles of surviving
snow, grey with
exhaust.

The long wooden loungers
are a Goliath's prone throne
next to the feeble chairs
that sink like a parabola
under the strength
of my (m)ass.

The long wooden loungers are
mostly occupied by white girls
talking of tanning, despite
the grey winter sky.
I'm bumped and trip (bad
knee) by a sidewalk jock
with a prohibited
Frisbee.

The long wooden loungers
hold Coral and I for a while.
I get a peeling red sunburn,
as if the loungers made it
Summer.

Blur

The trio of architects who reincarnated the High Line
built a structure out of steam in Switzerland.

A *tensegrity* structure, the Blur Building was a nothing
Rising out of Lake Neuchatel's waters.

Its light mobile surface encased structural rods,
which were brittle. Stretched-taffy surface emanating a cloud.

The Blur Building was outfitted with a "smart" weather system,
which was equipped with thirty-five thousand water nozzles.

This system recorded information about its milieu each second
and then produced the requisite amount of mist to create a cloud.

This cloud was the only thing a visitor could see.
They could wade into the building, which seemed to hover—

built of its environment,
its vaporized nature.

Blur was an illusion of stable structure produced
by constant movement; by infinite droplets running in and out

of a self-recycling cloud; by the insubstantiality
of this architecture, its malleability,

its continual transformations posed as *form*,
its gender, its transgender, its body.

The World Without Us

Alan Weisman wrote a book all about
Manhattan's undercurrents, the secret rivers
over which millions pavement-pound daily;
on this island, ground is just a middle point.

The author prophesies that
Nature will soon answer.

It's already happening: subway tunnels flood often;
hurricanes smash cities into room-temp bodega-diets;
roller coasters unhinge; you go to the theatre
to charge your cell phone with a generator.

The author claims that the High Line
used to be the best example of this:

there, repressed Nature returned, unbidden,
to make worlds on the booty of an urban corpse.

Its wildness spelt out a message in disparate plant species. It
was legible to anyone high enough to see forests and not trees:

*You are not
in control.*

In Which Mother Nature Returns

Streamers of greens and vines
festoon off the High Line
Chokecherry branches
wrap around the neck
of the Chrysler Building
and squeeze.

Fulsome fields of poison ivy
slide down its rails like a sled
head over to Bill Clinton and
Tr*mp at their Harlem properties
creep up their legs like
a flirtatious under-table toe
and, for years, make them
scratch their own damn backs.

Black widow spiders, big as octopi
occupy Wall Street bankers,
sink their fangs into every
respectable, clean
shiny-smiled gay
who cries at Pride
but keeps the change
he doesn't need
when asked if he
could spare some.

Mother Nature,
on the High Line,
babysits a Venus flytrap
with a taste for urban developer penis.

It is a *vagina dentata* on a beanstalk
that mouths words to would-be friends:

> *good luck,*
> *suckers*

Vice/Virtue

Diller Scofidio + Renfro,
who redesigned the High Line,
once used their credit cards to make art
(years before their armloads of arts museums,
haute couture furnishings, and worldwide fame).

Soft Sell
began as a shame-shuttered porn theatre near Times Square.
They took this cracked canvas and projected a protest onto it:
life-large red lips that seemed to emit whispered propositions
to consuming passersby, window-gawkers.

Vice/Virtue
is a quad set of glassware, including:
a tumbler with built-in cigarette holder
and vortex for funneling smoke;
a champagne flute with a needle built into the stem;
a water glass with a cubby for prescription (or other) pills.

Bad Press
reshapes white dress shirts,
pressing them against the factory aesthetic
of the high-end man-blouse
in the name of "dissident ironing."

Past several years have seen them pitch
eighteen museums or arts centres worldwide
(Calgary, Alberta turned one down)

Vanity Chair
places a plucking mirror atop
a stick sharpened at both ends,
stabbed through the seat of the chair,
which leaves nowhere to sit and
no way to move.

Found: Audio Track from DS+R's Guerilla Installation Art, *Soft Sell*

Hey you, wanna buy
Hey you, wanna buy
Hey you, wanna buy
Hey you, wanna buy
Hey you, wanna buy
Hey you, wanna buy
Hey you, wanna buy
Hey you, wanna buy
Hey you, wanna buy
Hey you, wanna buy
Hey you, wanna buy
Hey you, wanna buy
Hey you, wanna buy
Hey you, wanna buy
Hey you, wanna buy
Hey you, wanna buy
Hey you, wanna buy
Hey you, wanna buy
Hey you, wanna buy

a second chance?
    an authentic, original, only one of its kind?
        some motherly love?
    an ivy league education?
    a ticket to paradise?
        your name in lights?
        a new suit that makes you look important?
        a rare opportunity?
        a left kidney?
            a judge?
a turbo-charged five-speed souped-up shiny red muscle car?
a vowel?
a place in heaven?
a one-year subscription?
an all-you-can-eat diet plan?
yourself some more time?
a brand new baby boy?
a new identity?
an unobstructed view of the skyline?
a place in history?

The Hard Sell

I teach a book about the porn theatres
of the old Times Square, of the way
in which people of different
social classes and races
and "lifestyles"
actually met
but not only
met but
even

TOUCHED [!!!]

each other in the dark,
under the cinematic glow
or maybe under the seats
and possibly beneath your
notice or your regard.

I have attended happenings
that were a sort of fleshy
requiem to these places
where the audience could not
feign distance from the show,
from the fact that bodies want,
and persist, and can enjoy
each other in ways that
make family become
something new
in the bones
and sinew.

Some might think that public touch is only
fun (and I ask: what have you against fun?)
but there are many types of fun and, moreover,
many types of non-fun that are crucial
to this thing that a professional
might call
"thriving."

Staff bored holes in the walls of the YMCA
to further negate the compromised "privacy"
of men having sex with men in the steam.
We can argue it with rigour a la Academe,
but this paper will argue that it's simpler
than it may, at first, seem:

Times Square was sanitized
because of a myth that
I encourage you
to hold in rather
extreme disesteem:
that hawking knock-off bags
is more important
than creaming
your jeans.

Plants & Animals

It's not Christmas time in Chelsea market yet.
They aren't hawking goose and meat-mince yet.

High Line's January Bloom is still to come;
don't see the Jet Trail Flowering Quince yet.

A mourning leatherman stings me with the sorrow in his eyes.
His cheeks shine meat-red but I haven't heard him wince yet.

Charlie Brown tree on the old High Line, lit.
Who crawled out there and was she drinking nog?

> You square-danced with a stranger in Chelsea
> but have not seen her eastside strut since. Yet . . .

Go Back to Northern California
and Take Your Science With You

Assignment at Columbia University:
map something you see on the High Line, and
represent it visually in a way that matters to you.

A young affianced woman
drew families, couples   couples, families
A banker drew himself looking into the sky.
I drew interlocking triangles everywhere
that I saw queerness.

> (Yes, it's humble, humble pie,
> professor. But it's no less a fantasy
> than the family form or your certainty.)

I freehand a network of triangles to resemble the slices
of fabric that meant you were likely to die in the Holocaust.

At the deli nearby, an age-faded poster
of a pastrami sandwich sits sideways
in the window, a fatty pink isosceles.

An aged *for-lease* sign on a shuttered-up shop
that might have once been
Dizzy Izzy's bagels.

Sex-segregated toilets marked by the sharp triangled
iconography of a woman in a dress remind me
of David Wojnarowicz's lips sewn shut.

I sat with the professor

Her: blond, beige,
              peach, narrow

Me: purple glitter, paisley hanky,
           pierced, wide, pained

She said: *well, how can you tell if something is queer—*
It's hardly a scientific process!

She's right, it's counter-scientific. I said:
Well, there is *a queer aesthetic.*   (*Many*, I thought.)

She told me to redo the assignment.
I cruised home with pastrami-pink fire in my belly, burning
about this era in which we let
straight Californians define queerness

      as an imperceptibility,
      as a body they are proud *not* to see.

      Her High Line requires tunnel vision, can't abide a freak.
      My High Line creeps up on us, swerves left, is oblique.

H,i,g,h,L,i,n,e

I- I-   high line
     i i
          i i

Hi Lie Line Hen Leg Gin Gel
Gig Gil Nil Ile Heil Nile
High Heel Hill Gill
Line Liege
                    Hi Line
                    Hi Li
                    i i

            i i   High Line Aisle I

        i i

                    i i

                    I lie

                    I—

Found: High Line Plant Species that Sound Pretty Queer

Wavy Hair Grass

Smooth Aster   Stiff Aster

Giant Pussy Willow   Himalayan Sweetbox

Flameleaf Sumac   Forest Pansy Redbud

Pinus Virginiana   Clusterhead

Spiked Gayfeather   Pink Delight Meadow Sage

Glory-of-the-Snow

Fatal Attraction Coneflower

Keep It Wild: Keep It On the Path

A placard blocking
the unruly arteries
of the park:

> *KEEP IT WILD*
> *KEEP IT ON THE PATH*

Clashing commands legislated a
double-decade too late

> "It" has slid from us to plants
> from ass to grass

The path leads somewhere
someone else has been

Makes us walk as
alphabetic automatons

> getting from point A to
> point B to A, B, A, B, C, C

> To agree never to touch something—
> Is that to keep anything at all?

Yet, the park's concrete planks
point you against the grain
You walk straight but they
veer off, end, start anew

> If you pay attention to this
> suddenly it becomes
> difficult to walk
> sober-straight

If you sit down dizzy
and high, the park
has taught you

how to approach a floor slantwise

exorcising grace
a posture of hesitation
an out-of-line pelvis   feral hipbone
                                         tripped-out toes

a spiked-spine that knows
to go where no path . . .

FOUND: High Line Plant Species that Sound like Drag Names

Lady in Black Calico-Aster

The Rattlesnake Master   The Southern Gentleman

        Grace Smokebush

                Brandywine Smooth Witherod

        Walter Funcke Yarrow

                Ruby Tuesday Sneezeweed

        Jim Dandy Winterberry

Horatio Goatsbeard

Harlequin Glorybower

A Yellow Elevator is Not a Submarine

But I'd live in it somewhere between
first and second floor as a splinter.
I'd set up shop in a cross-section incision
to live amidst the bumpy ugly guts
and gassy burps of *Architecture.*

Ascending to the High Line
is a trip in a transparent yellow box
named by corporate paint purveyors
"Sick Grass" or "Buttered Urine," perhaps.

The elevator is not a submarine but I'd take it to the
deep sea to see if it would, then, seem green to me.

I'd take it into the deep sea with some whiteboard pens
to write some A, B, A, B, C, C poetry on the walls
until the elevator is opaque with verse and the coast guard
thinks I'm a black box from a giant's airplane,
one of those records of disaster that's only useful too late.
I'd be an archive-grave beneath the waves.

Hello, yellow elevator that fades my view of Jersey.
You're so smug about the way you make the whole world
look old like newsprint, a dim bulb, or a ring around a collar.
It's as if, stepping out, the High Line restores us to the present,
to the future yet to come—
                              you're not a yellow box;
                              you're the green room!

You're too transparent
for me to pick my nose in you.
You're not a submarine but
I'd have a rough first kiss
held up against you.

(Trumpets Play)

Rejected High Line Sitcom Pitch #7

Near Columbia,
at the Hamilton Deli at Amsterdam and 114ᵀᴴ,
there's a sandwich called the Fatboy, and
when I speak the word, it is not so much
an order as a proclamation of self.

Near the High Line,
there's a red faux-retro deli that carries
concrete blocks of mock chicken and
ninety-nine cent cherry pies
that don't need an icebox.
Sun-sprawled on the bottom rack of sat-fat snacks
is a white and orange tabby who spends her days
stretching and sleeping from salt & vinegar to barbecue.

Two entirely other delis, both near the High Line,
are engaged in a delicate linguistic debate.
Two sandwich men set up shop, and each
wants to name their shop
after the High Line.

This is the truth.
But is it also a sitcom for
the gentrified meat market?

Upon spying each other's signs, one man plants
fake roaches on the deli-counter of the other man,
who retaliates with clandestine calls to the New York City
Department of Health and Mental Hygiene to make
fictitious complaints. Each deli ends up with a c sanitation
rating perched in its front window and both are eventually
shuttered up. One day, to drown out the acrid taste of
just desserts, each heads to his favourite bar to watch
his favourite baseball team lose. They end up elbow-to-elbow
at the same place same time same same same. They seal
a deal with drunk sunrise back-slaps and slur out an
announcement to other bar patrons that they are launching
a new collaborative joint: THE UNITED HIGH LINE DELI

Cue Theme Music

Steal this pitch if you like. It's not always clear
who owns what, and why, and how, anyways.

By the time you steal it, there'll be a new
"new neighborhood"   and someone else to chase
                                    the fat boys and cool cats
                                    away.

The Gansevoort Hotel, 2008

A coma economy is a way
to afford a trip to NYC.

Each time I entered the hotel,
the concierge wanted my ID.

(The damage deposit
was bigger than me.)

[CONTEXT 1: the city let you grow taller than that
mandated by the neighbourhood's new heritage status.]

History weighs on us as inevitability, but
even architects know it's a rather arbitrary plan:

[CONTEXT 2: you were named after a market named
after a street named after a military man.]

You are rose petals stomped
in the hall on Valentine's Day.

You are free champagne
drained down the toilet.

You are the woman in
the indigo dress sobbing.

Pasts are plural. I try
to remember this often.

Tensegrity

Tensegrity is
a portmanteau
of tensional integrity.

It describes a
bipartite structure:

      1. a thin, light outer façade, and,
      2. inner rods running in all directions.

The stretchy façade hugs itself inwards, and
the rods push this membrane outwards,

such that
structure exists
only because of tension,
only because
of the structure's
contrary forces,
its dual desires
to both express
and in-press.

[CONTEXT 1: the Blur Building is a tensegrity structure.]

[HYPOTHESIS 1: human bodies are tensegrity structures too.]

This is a tension
that bids buildings
to stand tall
without the
fascism of gravity,

without the intransience
of concrete or the
monumental drive
of a skyscraper.

This is foundation-free,
refusing immobility.

This is one way of building new things
with the beautiful brute that we could,

in a newly gendered world,
call wrecked integrity.

Head of the Class, Columbia Architecture

My classmate wears a suit from Milan,
performs an Upper East Side attitude,
wears shoes that grew in a bayou, and
a shirt starched by hired arms.
His glossy briefcase reflects the world.
He fancies himself a *Savile Row* savant,
a bespoke Howard Roark.
He wet-dreams of himself
curling his toes around
a cliff's edge, gazing
into the sky of his
boundless future.

He is on leave from Wall Street
to take this undergraduate course
to "groom himself" into an architect
so that he can "leave his mark" on the world.
I picture his penis on steroids
or pumped up with air from its
shriveled state, set hard in concrete
painted lichen-grey and green
to look old, immortal.

We are tasked with a collage: cut up
the High Line, humpty-dumpty,
glue together every shard-shell
in some new way, into some good egg
    He takes a single photograph
    of his view of the horizon, off the park—
    to represent his "new direction
    and future as an architect"
    he does one shot, one take
    copies, pastes, copies, pastes
    copies, pastes—fifty times.

The professor's
feedback:
        Oh, wow, I really *appreciate*
        the restraint you've used here!

To the Board of Directors of
Friends of the High Line:

Befriending a piece of architecture is almost
certainly possible, but can you reclaim friends
by fiat or by pressing a fifty into a palm
disguising the gesture as a handshake?

> In a friend's hospital room, will you hide
> the "Do Not Resuscitate" sign?
> Or are you able to let go of the part
> of yourself that resides in that bed?

At a wake, will you kiss a rubber-dead wrinkled cheek?
Or will you pull the lever at the crematorium?

Do you sit up, warm milk and whiskyed, writing a eulogy
and wondering how—*if*—a life can be postscripted?

In what manner do you pursue the necessary failure
of speaking in the voice of a lost other?

Befriending a piece of architecture is perhaps
possible, but do you know how to grieve?

Is there some corner of the
High Line you forgot to clean?

Some crevice you are not able to see
where a spider web grows like a veil?

III.

A Kaleidoscope, A Mirage, A Self

Year 2039: The High Line Becomes a Live-In Mall

On this incarnation of the High Line, "Aisle 1"
will hide all the relics of this bad old 2018 world.

> *Paging Elizabeth to Aisle 1, Elizabeth to Aisle 1*

> *We're out of lower-realm root vegetables*
> *and down-there extra-long fishing line!*

Those chosen few who will ascend
will never have to come down to Earth.
They will never touch a hand that touched
the planet. They will never hear of express trains.

Their transit will be by air cab, a cloud-car that'll go as far as
the rail yard at the North and 14TH Street at the South.

The chosen will think it's a less painful purgatory, just
a stopover between dear daddy's penthouse and god.

> But who will work the registers, sell the stamps,
> and fix the plumbing when the septic tubes crack
> with frozen slop in the cold of February?

The ascendants will send bumbling old land-buses
to Queens to pick up ground-workers who will be
issued moon-shoe slippers and high-altitude pills.

I don't know what future-me will do
when the High Line morphs again . . .

Roll into a ball and hide behind the
pancake stack of yoga mats in Aisle i?

Or, in 2039, will I lie, citing a fat blue lazy
eye that makes me too tipsy up high?

No, on architectural apocalypse day,
I'll just keep breathing as usual:
a cycle of gasp and sigh

      hoping physics still applies
      and that only hot air will rise.

Parkour 1

Old kids climbed onto the High Line for years, with
upper-body strength and a strong disregard for rules.
I imagine so many Batmen without a purpose
not so much flying as gliding up.
The all-important art of leverage:
      using your tight spot
      to force yourself
      elsewhere.

At a strip club in Montreal
hard-armed white boys
dance the pole and
stroke soft cock on stage
for seven onlookers   (buyer's market).
So many seemed to want the body who
leveraged himself into a
human flagpole
marking the stage as his.

Yes, his. Tenuous property.
No timid proprieties here.

Parkour
uplifts.

But land and flags
are flaccid bedfellows.

Other Death Avenues I

Online reviews of the High Line
often mention that AIDS
wiped out "the transsexuals"
and the meat market's sex clubs.

"Wiped out" as if the
people are the germs.
As if we're discussing
a dirty cupboard, a sponge
and the studly bottom named
Mr. Clean.

My generation sees the photos:
faces bruised from the inside out;
bird bones in skin clothes;
memorial quilts that leave you cold.

We imagine being
at St Patrick's cathedral
with thousands of others;
we imagine what
the church floor
would feel like
if we laid on it.

We wonder
what string
in us would
be plucked
if we watched that protestor
snap a wafer of holy communion
and drop it to the floor
like scrap paper—
breaking bread.

Another Binary

Low Road   High Line
Low Life   High Five

    Low Maintenance
    High Strung
            Lowball   Highball
            Low Key   High Pressure

     high hat
     high horse
     high heel

low carb   high fibre
low sugar   high protein
low fat   high iron

    Low blow
    Low Brow
           Low Dose   Highfalutin

    High Waisted Jeans
    Low Hanging Fruit

      low down high school

      low-fi high-art

        Low Road

        High High Line

A Picture of Me on the High Line, August 2009

One day, in the intensive Architecture studio
that I'd soon drop, I was distracted by others' phobias

and the blade slipped, slicing my
fingertip off. Accidental crime-scene.

After Emerg, I wandered, lonely,
Percocet-high, trailing blood behind.

I bought a pink t-shirt three sizes too small,
some strong cheese, no crackers.

In my bed, I giggled, an amateur with drugs. I felt
that I could see my own nose for the first time.

I tucked a slice of gorgonzola into my top desk drawer,
thinking I had put it away. I booked a ticket to go back to her,

left hours later, after tossing watermelon rinds
on the floor and leaving no note for my roommate.

> The morning this photo was taken,
> we gathered my things at Columbia at 6 AM.

> Nothing had been touched, not even
> the dry thick chip of my fingertip,

> which clung to my sketchbook,
> haloed by a quarter-sized stain,
> a readymade watercolour of loss.

This picture of me on the High Line
recalls those ghost-chaser TV shows
where the photographic evidence
is a light outline—a hollow body

that may be attributed to just
a minute change in temperature.
These shapes only hint at a presence
of an absence we'd be scared to find

The way my hand was bandaged,
I couldn't wipe my ass.
I learned to use the other hand;
I have never been able to revert.

Artist's Statement

APPLICATION #46575869
DATE: 17 September 2018
NAME: Brandywine Smooth Witherod

I named myself after a plant on the High Line.
It's navy and magenta berries all clusterfucked at the tip
of the branch, like the stolen red-and-blue molecule-models
I made into a glittered crib-mobile in high school.

You have no business in my pants, but I wear blush
and blue-eyeshadow with the smoky-eye effect because
everybody should know that I'm on fire. I stomp the line
between "cross-dressing" and cross-living. Oh, that line—
thin as a G-string sometimes. And as uncomfortable.
[QUESTION 1: from *what*, exactly, am I imagined to be
"crossing"?]

I believe we live in a chloroformed culture, like we've
all forgotten how to breathe. But me, I sing—silently—even
when I don't know the words. Lipsunk on stage: *motherfucker*
watermelon motherfucker watermelon motherfucker
watermelon, etc. These two words can fill the mouth of
any other word if you will it.

METHODOLOGY: exaggerating one's own mistakes in
art allows for a consideration of the role of the vulnerable.
Or maybe just—the show must go on, go on.

EXPERIENCE: I work at a call centre too. That is why
I would like this grant. I am tired of soothing babies who are
angry that their high-speed internet is taking them nowhere
fast. I would choose any old song over that *9 to 5* every
damn day. The only way you can pay cover at *my* show
is to leave your cell and yourself at the door.

I named myself after navy and magenta berries
that are art-school sexy on the arms of a plant. I cultivate
a city acre of them on my fire escape and water them
with the dregs of my wine.

I make bodies and plants into collage but at heart
I'm not a crafter. Rather, I get hard for hybrids; I'm a rock-star
grifter grafter who you just might find hanging, hanging,
hanging from your rafters.

Found: Queer Urban Superiority Complex

Whatever our sensibility
may be, New York gays are
justifiably proud of
their status as tastemakers
for the rest of the country

Our clothes
and haircuts   our clothes
and records   and haircuts
and dance steps   and records
and décor—our
        restlessly evolving style—
        soon enough to become theirs—
                                Theirs
In return for the costliness   Our
and inconvenience, the squalor
and discomfort of our lives,
                We get to participate in whatever is the latest.
                We are never left out of anything
                We know what's happening.

Other Death Avenues II

I sat rapt in Hollywood, in love
with an original ACT-UP member
who was telling me about locking staffers
inside the NY Stock Exchange, while others
hung a banner and chained themselves
to the VIP balcony to protest
the cost of HIV drug AZT.
What happens when these stories
become good stories? How many times
will his throat instinctively form the words
like smoker's cough? I miss him.

High Liner

An old Canadian ad shows crotchety Captain High Liner
and a young blonde boy as his first mate. A Nor'Easter
rumbles the craft and the Cap'n's eyes
are like white-hot pokers when he asks
Ever been out to sea, Billy?
Or is this your first time?

Years later, Cap'n High Liner came
ashore and traded up to tumble-rough
Cap'n Morgan. They met
at the Mineshaft and argued
over whether a blow-fish or a
one-eyed salmon would make
a better dinner guest.

Push came to shove
came to coming.

They are not going to hire a surrogate.
They're meant to be the last two of a ghost breed.

They are old now, phased out by cartoons.
Dazed on the High Line, gazing at the Hudson,
at a river that is fisherman- and pirate-free.

Morgan's peg leg dangles down, and
High Liner is empty-flask frisky.

He props Morgan up against the fence,
plops his Cap'n hat on his lover's greyed head,

crouches over and sucks the peg leg
until his every lick is a splinter, because

all memory is prosthesis and desire is
already a ventriloquist, hands-free.

Parkour II

Failing at parkour? Par for the course!
Elementary school gym class:
four "rope days" per half-year course.
That's when gravity grabbed me around the collar,
scuffed me up good, not for the first
but for one of the the worst times.
Mom would sit sideways on my bed
and I'd whisper her my worries
that tomorrow would be a rope day
as though she had a higher power of absolution.
Did she?
Other days she'd sit, and, desperate
for a witness, I'd talk to her until
she'd have to go to bed herself.
One day she suggested:
well just keep talking after I go
and I DID
Now I rehearse poems alone
but I can't be sure there's still
someone listening
on the other side of the door.

Other Death Avenues III

At new millennium sex parties
in condemned houses and art lofts
I watch people lightly jerk each other
with double-latex-wrapped hands,
or grind through two pairs of boxers.
Mourning can only fail
but I don't understand
this science of inclusion,
this performed *future perfect* tense:
the wish to have been in danger,
which is not to imply that safety
is possible, accessible, or
preferable, or knowable.

Erasure: Breaking Up

I don't understand.
I thought every morning was our first.
And now what? Trapped
in a sick Sunday?

Come over.
Never say shame.
We run.
We can't run.

Look how proud they are to come—
heavy hemorrhaging, pining.

I point at big (huge)
unfinished men.

Get a loft, cut off heels (fierce, rough, red).
Thrift-dig, buried hand.

Hold anything bad for you. Start crying.
Cut me. I'd like to get through.

Between you and I,
I should try something new—
a night's sleep, an orgasm,
taxpayer shit, home.

Uptown man, entitled.
Stop yourself before you—

Move on.
Why?

I'm wondering
I'm trying
I'm obsessing

Pineapple and
champagne
destiny.

Where?

Parkour III

We sang a song
at our student government conferences   (was a nerd)
about a needing to get across a forest.

The protagonist met with verses of obstacles:
river, dark, woods, a bear.

I couldn't go over it.
I couldn't go under it.
I couldn't go around it . . .
REFRAIN: *I had to go right through it!*

I see now it's just a rural legend—
a flat-foot tall-tale about the virtues
of linearity and accepting the terms
by which others decorate the world.

All of the supposed methods of shirking responsibility
can actually be deadly perfect strategies:
waiting, avoiding, exceeding, subverting.

> Parkour doesn't exist, even. Nobody passes
> steep slopes or locked coffers truly alone.

> Parkour was about freedom, they said.
> They use it to train the marines now.

Other Death Avenues IV

At an artsy bathhouse event,
the only people loosening their ties
or their zippers were the big people,
the sublime gnarly brutes, and the others
who have learned that to fight
anything is to fight it
with a public body.

The others gaped and gossiped
and gym-thin boys busied themselves
by taking prohibited photographs
to post on the internet without
consent or thought.

One of them really likes
Buck Angel, though . . .

QUESTION 1:
what does it mean
to raise money for bodies
you'd never ever touch?

What would he have done in the 80s,
if he were gay and of-age in New York?

Masturbating bachelor? Homophobe?
Defender of The Mineshaft dress code?

QUESTION 2:
for whom is the body private
and do they know all that they sacrifice
by avoiding every bit of pain they can?

To Measure Time Sideways

The Broadway musical about AIDS
features a coutured cast rhapsodizing
about how to measure a year in:

> daylight; sunsets; midnights;
> cups of coffee; inches; miles;
> laughter; strife; love; love; love;
> love; love; love; truths that she
> learned; times that he cried;
> bridges he burned; the way that
> she died; love; love; love; love;
> love; love; love; love;

In the Broadway musical about AIDS,
only one character dies:

> the Dominican cross-dresser [?]
> (who takes off "his" [?] wig during
> all intimate and important moments)
> who played drums on the street
> (and I suspect that is a code
> for sex work). But don't worry
> about the actor because he's done
> alright; he played a pedophilic
> piano teacher on *Law & Order SVU*
> last year. I can't say whether or not
> he's made a living . . .

The saved heterosexual woman reunites
with her heterosexual man and they
are the token of the future.

A poem about a public park is written
by trans fingers trying different rhythms,
guided by:

> the thought that comes to mind
> when you're falling; dizziness;
> the friction of three snow-crystals
> joining each other mid-air; helium;
> where you're looking after you've
> been slapped; magnets repelling
> each other; avalanche; eclipse;
> stop-motion animation; the feeling
> between leaving the dentist and
> eating for the first time; build-up;
> tear-down; change; survival; survival
> as change; change as survival;
> waves.

I Lie on the High Line

I.

I never went to the High Line or sucked transgender clit
or dick. I never asked for three free samples at Milk Bar's
lower eastside locale; it's just that I never find enough to lick.

I never asked a stranger to pull over his car so I could take
a hot dump in the woods. I never took off my old white panties
to use as toilet paper and even if I wanted to

abandon them in that forest and go home dirty-commando,
I don't know that I could. I never went to sex parties; I never
broke my finger getting penetrated on a broken table.

I never ran a marathon in Ireland because though my limbs
always survive, they are petrified and are not all that able. I
never got a Hot Richard from Betty Grable and I never

stole the concept of a "Hot Richard" from *30 Rock* or
learned who Betty Grable was from *Community*. I never
flipped over a lecher-professor's table and signed it with

my friends. I never say "The End" when I finish a story
because I know, I know, I know things can never end. I never
rage when I realize I've merely rhymed a word with itself.

I never bent over to tie my shoe and farted. I've never left
a kind person broken-hearted in Halifax or given flack to
those who hoard bric-a-brac while subletting my apartment.

I never know best. I usually do worse than you'd expect.
I never crowed at anyone to come out of the closet. I never
laughed at their mothers for being rich snotty fuckers

with an exceedingly low tolerance for anything worthwhile.
I never let a friend extract all my back's blackheads. I
never blueballed anybody or believed in that concept or

masturbated to the opera *Bluebeard*. I've never been
weird; I've never been fat; I've never worried the back
of my neck looks like a pack of hot dogs.

I've never had a dick and never put it in you. I never, ever,
really know what to do but I never let that stop me. I didn't
laugh when you told me you peed in a yogurt cup when my

roomie was in the shower. I didn't go see all the *Twilight*
movies by myself; I'm not the Captain of Team Jacob. I never
tried on Mom's special occasion make-up.

I never find pus charming. I never take too many headache
pills. I still have never, but I likely will, eat more than my fill
at a sushi buffet and barf a nori yarn-ball later that day.

I never play mental Tetris. I never type out what you're saying
with my fingertips against my jeans. I've never been lean,
mean, a Bacardi Breezer-guzzler, or a Prayer Machine.

I never use my Pay-Per-View service to order Karaoke
and sing to myself all night. I didn't order Girls Night Out,
Pure Shania, Madonna Classics, or anything of the sort.

I never was pregnant with Jesus. I never cried,
abort, abort, abort, abort! I never read a poem about
someone who was in the audience. *Psych*!

I never biked to a high school hockey game. I never dreamt
of gay jocks self-destructing on ice. I'd never hold up crude
posters about the other team. That would not be nice.

I have never fucked people who want to be straight.
What would be the point? I was never anointed by holy oils
by holy men in holy places through the haze of a holy joint.

I never saw young
dead Father Dan
in my dreams.

I never laughed when I met my mom's priest with his
white shorts, white belt, and handsome companion-man.
I never was a heretic bent over in hysterics when

Mom said the priest was on his way to a sabbatical in
San Fran. I never brainstormed a eulogy for someone who
hadn't died. I watched *The Muppets* but no I did not cry.

I hurt you, and you me, but
I do not tell a lie when I say
it's not because we tried to.

II.

I never didn't go to the High Line. I never chose not to take
a Percocet with a large bag of Cheezies. I never failed to
not be easy. I've never binged. I've never not purged. I did

not slice my finger off, so I never did not go to Emerg. I've
never hated the word "perv" and I never missed a pedestrian
by one small swerve. I never didn't secretly think that you have

a personality disorder. I never didn't judge your drinking. I've
never had a cavity search at the border. I've never regretted a
hasty Subway order and I've never eaten for three. I've never

not refused to make do with too few black olives on
a foot-long and I've never expected anything or
anyone, including me, to be or to feel "free."

I never am unannoyed by the imperative to be happy, by
the belief in utter truth, by the smell of my colostomy,
or by the lie that I have a colostomy.

I've never prevented anyone from not being close to me,
which means I never stop you from seeing too much
of what I don't want you to not want to see.

I never memorized "To Be or Not To Be" and I never didn't
disidentify with every single letter of LGBT. I never played
pool at the dyke bar. I could never find a cue.

I never jerked off on a full bus with
a Cosmo mag. I never promised
that every word would be true.

I never rely on my inability not to lie when I stand on the High
Line. I never pen lines without a doubt as to how they'll
turn out or if someone will recite one when I die.

I never thought that you, High Line,
needed to know "who I am"—
only that I never, ever, lie.

Other Death Avenues v

In the 1850s, Death Avenue casualties
were spectacularly flattened
in public, by thunder-loud
    lightning-quick
    technology.

Our Death Avenue
is a guilt-slow street studded with
the quiet coffin-nail queries
    of how to live
    with something
                most of us didn't   quite
                or did   quite
                or didn't quite
                live with.

EPILOGUE

Indigestion 1

In 1997,
Elizabeth Diller and Ricardo Scofidio,
    before abridging the High Line,
    before designing haute-couture lamps,
    and eighteen arts centres and museums,
came to the Banff Centre for the Arts.

They created an early virtual-reality piece,
a dining scene called "Indigestion:"

        a table with a film of a "dinner"
        projected on it from above;

        two sets of hands moving
        through the rites of supper;

        beside the table sat a touch-screen
        that let viewers enter the meal.

In 2012,
I am at the Banff Centre for the Arts   for the Arts
to make art about their High Line Park.

But I am just
the one doggy-paddling the pool every night at 8:45;
the one eating butter chicken room service as I write;
the one who only eats at the meal hall once a day;
the one with gender- and tummy-trouble both.

Did Liz and Ric *also* spend the
sleepy hours of bracing Banff nights
renovating mealtime strategies,
doubled-over sick between stanzas?

I am the one leaving meetings early to be ill   (for the Arts).

Did we all   Liz, Ric, and Me

      know that digestion is always more,
      much more, than a metaphor?

I was the one who ate too much gelato on
the High Line after the washroom had closed.

Indigestion II

I made a friend in Banff. We ate caramel apples
from one of Banff's nostalgic sweet shoppes.
Pop rocks; fun dips; nerds; b-b-bats;
confections resembling cigarettes.

Taste of a time when my tongue didn't seek
other tongues or lash itself later, after too much
meal-hall meat that was dry as the sound
of a hand hitting a bear skin stretched.

My friend told me that years ago,
an artist here made vast lollipops,
wonky treats to plant in the landscape
at the Banff Centre for the Arts.

She planted them on long white sticks
in the Rocky Mountain green. It was only
the black bears who bellied up
for a noon-time treat.

We found a box of cereal at one of Banff's sugar shacks,
a limited-time subsidiary of *Count Chocula*.
Its name is *Boo Berry*. Marshmallows and
machine-punched pink kibble.

I didn't like it as a kid—
I always preferred toast.

I behold the box of Boo Berries in Banff.
I'm still not sure about eating ghosts.

Scavenger Hunt

Locate an epigraph that reads, "this book isn't about me,
but it is; it perhaps is, and certainly isn't, about you, too."

Find a history test that straddles the binary of
FALSE OR TRUE OR FALSE OR TRUE OR FALSE OR TRUE!

The voices in this book are not fake
just because I might have made them up

Raise your hand if you know that
fantasy is a way to save your own life.

[QUESTION 1: what is more
front-line than a feeling?]

Wink if you know there is no unstoried self,
that truths are built too. Concretely.

Find the cells of you
that need to know, know, know.

Find a High Line plant gone to seed;
find two buds set to blossom and grow.

Describe ten ideas with which you disagree.
Brainstorm so you can build something better.

Frame a picture of your favourite dissenter.
Generate a 4-D map that shows us how to be tough, but gentler.

Find a redefinition of the concepts of property and propriety.
Make a world in which you just might stop and say hi to me.

Underline fifty-seven times you
thought my rhymes were too easy.

Highlight an asthmatic fatty on the
High Line who's getting too wheezy.

Circle: a line that's pure schmaltz; a stanza that's cheesy; a
poem that eschews sentiment; one that makes you queasy.

Smile at a transgender artist in the meatpacking district.
Flash a security camera on the High Line.

Make a new approach to nostalgia.
Design an experiment in dis/connecting from/to the past.

Find everyone who knows they are
neither the first nor the last.

Be a heart willing to run
nowhere, feral-fast.

I will meet you
there, outside.

Acknowledgements

I wish to thank several people at the University of Calgary Press: Brave & Brilliant series editor, Aritha van Herk; my editor Helen Hajnoczky for her wisdom, rigour, and patience; Melina Cusano for her beautiful cover design; Alison Cobra for her stellar work in promoting the book; and the two anonymous peer reviewers for their effort and their suggestions.

This book was drafted at the Writing Studio at the Banff Centre for the Arts in 2012. Thank you to Karen Solie and Tim Lilburn, who read and commented on the first draft.

I undertook the research for this collection as a SSHRC postdoctoral fellow at McGill in 2012-2013. I send many thanks to my supervisor, Dr. Annmarie Adams, who has supported the architectural studies of this literature nerd for some time now. Thank you to my "Introduction to Sexual Diversity" students, by whose enthusiasm I was inspired to think and to write.

Kindest thanks to the friends and family who supported me during the writing, revision, and publication of this book, including, but not limited to: Carmen Ellison, Derek Warwick, Janis Ledwell-Hunt, Jen Crawford, Joan Crawford, Marco Katz Montiel, Megan Morman, and Triny Finlay.

Ted Kerr, Susan Stryker, Shannon Webb-Campbell, and Annmarie Adams generously endorsed the book. I thank them for their time and care and for their own work.

"s,l,a,u,g,h,t,e,r,h,o,u,s,e,s, a,n,d, t,r,a,n,s,s,e,x,u,a,l,s," "Feel It for Yourself," and "Huddle, 24 May 2012" were published as part of a hybrid critical-creative piece in *Transgender Studies Quarterly* 1.4 (2014): 482-500.

"I Lie on the High Line" was published on *Plenitude* (on 13 Jan 2016). Thank you to Matthew Walsh for a very thorough and helpful edit on this poem.

An early version of "The World Without Us" appeared in *Lost in Thought* 6 (2013) as "The Time Has Come, the Walrus Said."

"FOUND: Mineshaft Dress Code" and "The Mineshaft" were published on *Chelsea Station* (on 19 August 2016).

Thank you to all of the reviewers, editors, and readers of these publications.

Notes

Think Like an Architect!—page 1

The High Line is an elevated train track that edges the western border of lower Manhattan. Seeds that are not indigenous to New York dropped from loose locomotive doors over the years. When the trains stopped running in the early 1980s, these seeds bloomed into an elsewhere-landscape, a flowery afterlife that commemorated dead commerce.

The Meatpacking District, through which the main sections of the High Line Park run, was brought to life by its mostly Black and Latinx residents, and was known for its early transsexual community, for AIDS activism, kink and leather clubs, and for a lively public life for queer youth—largely youth of colour. After sunsink, punks and urban adventurers hoisted themselves illegally onto the High Line to enjoy an unprecedented perspective on the Meatpacking District and the Hudson River.

After a very lengthy political and financial campaign, the High Line was restructured, redesigned and has reopened—phase-by-phase—as a public park, beginning in 2009. The original landscape was destroyed and then simulated with an ambitious planting schedule. No dogs or jogging are allowed on the long narrow space. In short order, Mom and Pop shops, diners, warehouses, and auto repair joints morphed into luxury hotels, haute cuisine eateries, and museums. As many sources indicate (including Citi Habitats' "Manhattan Residential Rental Market Report," 2015), the average rent for a studio apartment (550 square feet or smaller) in Chelsea is about $2300 USD, while a one-bedroom fetches about $3400 USD.

I write from a particular roll of the High Line's underbelly. I write as a rural, trans, queer, and white Jewish poet who has followed the High Line project closely for many years as a critic of architecture and urbanism. I cannot capture or represent the

trans and racialized lives lived there, yet I forgo the dangerous
illusions of distance and detachment. That is, while my project
here is poetic and not sociological, I do not pretend that my own
perspective and experiences do not inform my analyses of the
High Line. My view is not "objective," and the connections and
disconnections I share with New Yorkers, trans people of the
1980s and 90s, or queer urban planners are never fully knowable
or static. Rather, they are tenuous; they are both possible and
impossible, both urgent and futile, both real and imagined.

I write only from my limited perspective, with the hope that I
can direct readers to a wide variety of voices who speak, write, and
make art about the histories that the High Line (and the values
of "urban renewal" that undergird it) often conceal. My writing
derives from the experience of living in a metro-normative culture
and even a metro-normative queer culture and discourse; as
a rural person I am accustomed to not feeling like I am "from
anywhere." The way in which rural locales can and often are called
"buttfuck nowhere" gets at the possibly queer orientation to place
that this metro-normativity offers (if coercively) to small-town
queers and trans people (who, as many mainstream and queer
cultures would have it, need to move to a big city as a prerequisite
to commencing a real or livable life). I write, then, as a visitor to
New York who has had to live, always, with the city's power and
pull in media and queer imaginations.

My experience with the High Line has several facets. I lived
in Manhattan during the summer of 2009, during which time the
first phase of the High Line opened to the public. As a student of
an intensive "Introduction to Architecture" studio at Columbia
(a short-lived ivy-league experiment that I found transphobic,
ableist, ahistorical, and otherwise uninteresting), I was asked to

study this first phase of the park. While I studied the plans for the High Line before this time, and visited it many times after, I do draw from these experiences at Columbia for several poems.

Citi Habitats, "Manhattan Residential Rental Market Report" (New York, NY: City Habitats, 2015).

Section i. A Bone, A Tooth, A Ghost

Flagging Red—page 7

"Flagging" is the means by which some queer people indicate their sexual preferences, with the aid of coloured handkerchiefs in their back pockets. Each handkerchief indicates a certain sexual interest or fetish. For instance, a red handkerchief placed in the left back pocket indicates that the wearer like to fist others, while a red handkerchief placed in the right back pocket indicates that the wearer likes to be fisted.

Found: Daily Menu for the West-Side Cowboy on a Moderate Budget—page 11

This menu is assembled from Mrs. Putnam's recipes for west-side cowboys and diners on a diet.

Elizabeth H. Putnam, *Mrs. Putnam's Receipt Book and Young Housekeeper's Assistant* (Boston, MA: Ticknor, Reed, and Fields, 1850).

Found: On Not Looking Back—page 15

This poem is built of short, revised and reassembled quotations from the architecture-focused publications listed below that discuss the High Line. I have excerpted what I found to be the oddest mentions of transsexual people in order to show the weird way in which trans people are summoned up to represent the "seedy" past of the neighbourhood, as juxtaposed with the shiny new park.

Christian Bonetto, et al., *Discover New York City* (London, UK: Lonely Planet E-Books, 2012).

Barry Goldstein, "Small Hours in the Meatpacking District," *Gastronomica* 11 no. 4 (2011): 23-25.

Jaycess, "Hi from the High Line," TotalCliche.com (June 2019), http://jaycess-totalcliche.blogspot.ca/2009/06/hi-from-high-line_9858.html

Michael Klausner, "Living the High Line," *Day Tripper* blog for the *New York Times*, July 31, 2009 (page discontinued).

Karina Munoz, "New York's High Line and the Psychology of Urban Spaces," *Sunday Arts Blog* on *Thirteen: Media with Impact*, June 24, 2009, https://www.thirteen.org/sundayarts/blog/city/new-yorks-high-line-and-the-psychology-of-urban-spaces/723/

Joy Stocke, "On the High Line: Diamonds on the Soles of our Shoes," *Wild River Review* (May 2011), https://www.wildriverreview.com/columns/pen-world-voices/on-the-high-line/.

First Page of an Academic Article in Drag as a Poem
—page 17

This poem is made up of lines from my scholarly publication "A Transgender Poetics of the High Line Park" which details the transgender poiesis of the High Line.

Lucas Crawford, "A Transgender Poetics of the High Line Park." *Transgender Studies Quarterly* 1 no. 4 (2014): 482-500, DOI 10.1215/23289252-2815192.

This poem contains a reference to Christian Bonetto, et al., *Discover New York City* (London, UK: Lonely Planet E-Books, 2012).

s,l,a,u,g,h,t,e,r,h,o,u,s,e,s, a,n,d, t,r,a,n,s,s,e,x,u,a,l,s—page 19

Reviews of the High Line often note, with smirking derision, that the area used to be known for just its "slaughterhouses and transsexuals." It is this kind of violent linking of death, meat, and transsexuality to which this poem responds. Because "slaughterhouses and transsexuals" is such a succinct equation of the violence often found in architectural and urbanist reviews of the High Line, the poem uses only the letters found in this phrase.

Trans women are often, but not exclusively, the focus of such violent appraisals of the history of the High Line and its surrounding neighbourhoods. Relationships between transsexual women and cisgender heterosexual men take a wide variety of forms—this poem imagines just one of those forms. (This is not to suggest that the genders of the people in the poem are necessarily predetermined, clear, or obvious, but is, rather, to recognize that many of the transphobic accounts of the High Line area focus on sexual activity between cis-hetero men and women of trans experience, particularly sex workers.) I remain hopeful for the many types of mutually beneficial relationships that can exist between many different "categories" of person, if only because that hope, and the relationships it can generate, are so important to my own life.

Thank you to an anonymous peer reviewer at *Transgender Studies Quarterly* for asking me to think more about the variety of relationships that take place between identity categories and about the role of voice and authority in narratives of such relationships.

Bills, Bills, Bills—page 21

This poem references the artwork *The First $100,000 I Ever Made* by John Baldessari, displayed on the High Line Billboard in 2011.

John Baldessari, *The First $100,000 I Ever Made*, December 2–30, 2011, billboard, High Line, New York, NY, http://www.thehighline. org/blog/2011/12/02/high-line-billboard-qa-with-the-curator.

Found: The Mineshaft's Dress Code—page 33

The Mineshaft was a gay bar and sex club in the Meatpacking District, open from October 1976-November 1985. The club enforced a strict dress code, which was posted in a variety of forms over the years during which the club was in operation. This poem reproduces one version of the dress code with slight editorial changes. Reproductions of the dress code can be found online in the following locations:

"The Mineshaft Dress Code as Adopted by the Club on October 1, 1976," 78.media.tumblr.com, Accessed July 12, 2018, https://78.media.tumblr.com/86db660b472aa578684e8abe8ef7c217/tumblr_nrke38O8L51tzk69404_r1_1280.jpg

"Mineshaft NYC dress code, ca. 1979," JONNO.com, Accessed July 12, 2018, http://jonnodotcom.tumblr.com/post/116504128299/mineshaft-nyc-dress-code-ca-1979-via-the-golden

R.I.D. (A Response to Residents in Distress, *a late 1990s Neighbourhood Watch Group)—page 38*

In the late 1990s and early 2000s, new residents of the gentrifying lower west side united to form neighbourhood associations. These associations would patrol their neighbourhoods, scaring transgender and queer people of colour (especially youth) away from the social and communal spaces of these neighbourhoods, including sidewalks, parks, and street corners. This poem takes its name from one of these associations—R.I.D.—which stands for *Residents In Distress.* R.I.D. reportedly antagonized the queer and trans youth of colour on the sidewalks on streets of their neighbourhood.

For more context and information, please see Kenyon Farrow's article, "Making Change: a House of our Own," *City Limits*, March 15 2003, https://citylimits.org/2003/03/15/making-change-a-house-of-our-own/.

Section ii. A Blueprint, A Blade, A Branch

Found: Selected Plant Species on the High Line Park—page 47, and *Found: High Line Plant Species that Sound Pretty Queer—page 66*

These poems list plants that grow on the High Line. A complete list of the High Line's flora is available online:

Friends of the High Line, "High Line Plant List," last modified September 23, 2014, http://assets.thehighline.org/pdf/12_High%20 Line%20Plant%20List.pdf

Huddle, 24 May 2012—page 49

This poem is inspired by "Huddle," an ensemble dance performance choreographed by Italian-American artist Simon Forti. "Huddle" was first performed in 1961. As is described in the poem, "Huddle" consists of a group of six to nine dancers huddled together, with each dancer breaking free of the group in turn by climbing on top of the group, only to melt back into the huddle. In May 2012, Forti remounted Huddle specifically for a performance on the High Line.

Simon Forti, *Huddle*, performed May 24, 2012, New York, NY, from Friends of the Highline, "Simone Forti Huddle performance on the High Line," November 12, 2013, Youtube video, https:// www.youtube.com/watch?v=pf3X06xPjrE

The World Without Us—page 53

This poem takes its title from the Alan Weisman book of the same name, in which the author says that the pre-renovation High Line is a key example of the way in which nature can, and is already, reclaiming space from humans.

Alan Weisman, *The World Without Us* (New York, NY: St. Martin's Press, 2007).

Found: Audio Track from DS+R's Guerilla Installation Art,
Soft Sell—*page 58*

The architects who redesigned the High Line, DS+R, undertook a project in 1993 called "Soft Sell." As the architects explain on their website:

> Soft Sell is a video installation in the entrance to the Rialto, an abandoned porno theater on Forty-Second Street and Seventh Avenue. The project takes issue with the production of "desire" in relation to several forms of urban currency specific to the site: bodies, real estate and tourism. The video uses one of pornography's most familiar devices, the close-up, cut-up body. A pair of gigantic female lips, projected onto the entrance doors, recites a litany of solicitations to passerby. Her sensuous voice emanates from the original speak-hole of the ticket booth . . . With each demographic shift in the history of Forty-Second Street, the desire-producing apparatus adapts to accommodate and maintain a new currency. But whether the commodity be "the flesh" or "the fashionable," the strategy remains the same: the sustenance of any "object of desire" is dependent on its indefinite deferral.

For this found poem, I have selected some of the "solicitations" offered to audience members of "Soft Sell," as a way of asking DS+R and their fans (of which I am one) to imagine these feminist and anti-capitalist statements emerging from the High Line. With this new imagined context, it is possible to query the stark juxtaposition of DS+R's older projects with newer ones like the High Line, which seem to participate in urban renewal and gentrification in more straightforward fashion.

Poem printed with the permission of DS+R.

DS+R, "Soft Sell," accessed July 12, 2018, https://dsrny.com/project/soft-sell.

The Gansevoort Hotel, 2008—page 74

The New York City Preservations Commission established The Gansevoort Market Historic District in 2003. The Commission held tight to one exception to the new historic district rules, however: the forthcoming Gansevoort Hotel would not be subject to new limitations on vertical growth (ie. height of buildings). For more, see "Gansevoort Market Historic District Designation Report," listed in the "Further Reading" section.

To the Board of Directors of Friends of the High Line:
—page 79

The version of friendship that I imagine as possible in the face of the High Line draws more from Jacques Derrida's sense of the loss inherent to friendship, rather than the focus on salvation that underpins the emotional mode of those committed to the High Line as an urban project. Here is a sample of Derrida's thinking of this subject, from *Politics of Friendship*:

> The anguished apprehension of mourning (without which the act of friendship would not spring forth in its very energy) insinuates itself a priori and anticipates itself; it haunts and plunges the friend, before mourning, into mourning... This is the very respiration of friendship, the extreme of its possibility. Hence surviving is at once the essence, the origin and the possibility, the condition of possibility of friendship; it is the grieved act of loving.

Jacques Derrida, *Politics of Friendship* (Brooklyn, NY: Verso Books, 2005), 14.

SECTION III. A KALEIDOSCOPE, A MIRAGE, A SELF

Parkour 1—page 85

Parkour is the "the activity or sport of moving rapidly through an area, typically in an urban environment, negotiating obstacles by running, jumping, and climbing." The word comes from the French *parcours* for "course," and, in turn, from the Latin *per* (through) and *currere* (to run).

Oxford English Dictionary s.v. "Parkour," accessed July 12, 2018, https://en.oxforddictionaries.com/definition/parkour.

FOUND: *Queer Urban Superiority Complex—page 93*

This poem is composed of lines from *States of Desire Revisited* by Edmund White in an effort to explore the language used to capture gay New York identity, culture, and self-perception.

Edmund White, *States of Desire Revisited: Travels in Gay America* (Madison, WI: University of Wisconsin Press, 2014), 259-60.

High Liner—page 95

A "High Liner" is both an 1850s term for a fishing captain with a reputation of hauling in the best fish, as well as the name of "a leading North American processor and marketer of prepared, value-added frozen seafood."

"Company Overview," Our Company, High Liner Foods, accessed July 12, 2018, http://www.highlinerfoods.com/en/home/company/company-overview.aspx.

ERASURE: *Breaking Up—page 99*

The base text for this erasure poem is the script for an episode of *Sex and the City* entitled "Cock-a-Doodle-Do" which features Samantha, who has recently moved into the gentrifying Meatpacking District. Angered by the late night conversations of Black sex workers of transsexual experience (conversations that even the supposedly brazen and liberated Samantha finds crude), she undertakes a nasty campaign against these people with a longer history of attachment to the neighbourhood. This is especially ironic, given that Samantha's defining character trait on the show is her refusal to capitulate to various norms of propriety, especially those of sexual propriety. This poem responds to the violence of this episode by chopping and erasing the script itself, decentralizing Samantha and her concerns.

Sex and the City, season 3, episode 18 "Cock-a-Doodle-Do," written by Michael Patrick King, directed by Allen Coulter, created by Darren Star, aired October 15, 2000, on HBO, script accessed July 12, 2018, Sex and the City Transcripts, "318. Cock-A-Doodle-Do," http://www.satctranscripts.com/2008/08/sex-and-city-season-3-episode-18.html.

To Measure Time Sideways—page 103

My analysis of the High Line of history—its performance of temporality—relies on the theories of architectural critic Sanford Kwinter:

> When the modern clockface was invented, it allowed time to be dissociated ever further from human events, at once spatially projected in vision and displayed in a marvelously rationalized notational form . . . Clock time fixes in order to correlate, synchronize, and quantify, renouncing the mobile, fluid, qualitative continuum where time plays a decisive role in transformative morphogenetic processes . . . Time, forced now to express the false unity and rationality of all being, ceased to be real . . . Real time is more truly an engine, however, than a procession of images—it is expressed only in the concrete, plastic medium of duration. Time always expresses itself by producing, or more precisely, by drawing matter into a process of becoming-ever-different, and to the product of this becoming-ever-different—to this in-built wildness— we have given the name novelty.

Sanford Kwinter, *Architectures of Time: Toward a Theory of the Event in Modern Culture* (Boston, MA: MIT Press, 2002), 4-5.

Further Reading

The High Line, Architecture, and/or New York

Alemani, Cecilia, ed. *High Art: Public Art on the High Line*. New York: Skira Rizzoli, 2015.

Crawford, Lucas. "A Transgender Poetics of the High Line Park." *Transgender Studies Quarterly* 1, no. 4 (2014): 482-500. DOI 10.1215/23289252-2815192, Duke University Press.

Delany, Samuel R. *Times Square Red, Times Square Blue*. New York: New York University Press, 1999.

Diller, Elizabeth, and Ricardo Scofidio. *Flesh: Architectural Probes*. Princeton: Princeton University Press, 1998.

———. *Blur: The Making of Nothing*. New York: Harry N. Abrams, 2002.

Dimendberg, Edward. *Diller Scofidio + Renfro: Architecture after Images*. Chicago: University of Chicago Press, 2013.

Farrow, Kenyon. "Making Change: a House of Our Own." *City Limits*. March 15 2003. https://citylimits.org/2003/03/15/making-change-a-house-of-our-own/.

Friends of the High Line, eds. *Designing the High Line: Gansevoort Street to 30th Street*. New York: Friends of the High Line, 2008.

Sylvia Rivera Law Project. *"It's War in Here:" a Report on the Treatment of Transgender and Intersex People in NYS Men's Prisons*. New York: Sylvia Rivera Law Project, 2007. http://archive.srlp.org/resources/pubs/warinhere

Lindner, Christoph and Brian Rosa, eds. *Deconstructing the High Line: Postindustrial Urbanism and the Rise of the Elevated Park*. New Brunswick: Rutgers University Press, 2017.

Shockley, Jay. "Gansevoort Market Historic District Designation Report." New York: New York City Landmarks Preservation Commission, 2003.

Sternfeld, Joel. *Walking the High Line*. 3rd ed. Brooklyn: Steidl, 2012.

Related Theories and Histories of Transgender and/or Queerness

Chen, Mel Y. *Animacies: Biopolitics, Racial Mattering, and Queer Affect*. Durham, NC: Duke University Press, 2012.

Handhardt, Christina B. *Safe Space: Gay Neighborhood History and the Politics of Violence*. Durham, NC: Duke University Press, 2013.

Haritaworn, Jinthana, Ghaida Moussa, and Syrus Marcus Ware, with Río Rodríguez, eds. *Queering Urban Justice: Queer of Colour Formations in Toronto*. Toronto: University of Toronto Press, 2018.

Herring, Scott. *Another Country: Queer Anti-Urbanism*. New York: NYU Press, 2010.

Johnson, E. Patrick. *Appropriating Blackness: Performance and the Politics of Authenticity*. Durham, NC: Duke University Press, 2003.

Rubin, Gayle S. *Deviations: a Gayle Rubin Reader*. Durham, NC: Duke University Press, 2011.

Spade, Dean. *Normal Life: Administrative Violence, Critical Trans Politics, and the Limits of Law*. Durham, NC: Duke University Press, 2015.

Stanley, Eric, and Nat Smith. *Captive Genders: Trans Embodiment and the Prison Industrial Complex*, 2nd ed. Oakland, CA: AK Press, 2015.

Stryker, Susan, *Transgender History: the Roots of Today's Revolution*, 2nd ed. Berkeley, CA: Seal Press, 2017.

———. "Dungeon Intimacies: the Poetics of Transsexual Sadomasochism." *Parallax* 14, no. 1 (2008): 36-47.

Selected Transsexual, Transgender, Non-Binary, Two-Spirit, Genderqueer, and/or Queer Poetry

Belcourt, Billy-Ray. *This Wound is a World*. Calgary, AB: Frontenac House, 2017.

Benaway, Gwen. *Passage*. Owen Sound, ON: Kegedonce Press, 2016.

Blythe, Ali. *Twoism*. Fredericton, NB: Goose Lane, 2015.

Driskill, Qwo-Li. *Walking with Ghosts*. Norfolk, UK: Salt Publishing, 2005.

Franco, Tanis. *Quarry*. Calgary, AB: University of Calgary Press, 2018.

Latini, Lilith. *Improvise, Girl, Improvise*. Brooklyn, NY: Topside Press, 2015.

Salah, Trish. *Lyric Sexology Vol 1*. Montreal, QC: Metonymy Press. First published 2014 by Roof Books (New York).

———. *Wanting in Arabic*. 2nd ed. Toronto, ON: TSAR Publications, 2013.

Theonia, Charles. *Which One is the Bridge*. Brooklyn, NY: Topside Press, 2015.

Thom, Kai Cheng. *a place called No Homeland*. Vancouver, BC: Arsenal Pulp Press, 2017.

Tolbert, TC, and Trace Peterson, eds. *Troubling the Line: Trans and Genderqueer Poetry and Poetics*. Callicoon, NY: Nightboat Books, 2013.

Author on the High Line, 2009

LUCAS CRAWFORD is a poet and an associate professor of English literature at the University of New Brunswick. Lucas's previous poetry collection, *Sideshow Concessions* (Invisible Publishing), won the Robert Kroetsch Award for Innovative Poetry in 2015. Lucas's academic book, *Transgender Architectonics: the Shape of Change in Modernist Space* (Routledge, 2016), sparked an interest in the High Line Park and its histories. Lucas was awarded the 2019 Arcus/Places Prize, an honour given biannually by Berkeley's College of Environmental Design to scholars who write about gender, sexuality, and space. Lucas is from rural Nova Scotia.

BRAVE & BRILLIANT SERIES

SERIES EDITOR:
Aritha van Herk, Professor, English, University of Calgary
ISSN 2371-7238 (Print) ISSN 2371-7246 (Online)

Brave & Brilliant publishes fiction, poetry, and everything in between and beyond. Bold and lively, each with its own strong and unique voice, Brave & Brilliant books entertain and engage readers with fresh and energetic approaches to storytelling and verse, in print or through innovative digital publication.